Very Special Sacred Songs

Vocal • Piano • Guitar
Complete Sheet Music Editions

D1616342

©1993 Creative Concepts Publishing Corporation
All Rights Reserved
Catalog No. 07-1039
ISBN #1-56922-025-5

Exclusive Distributor:
CREATIVE CONCEPTS PUBLISHING CORPORATION
2290 Eastman Avenue #110, Ventura, California 93003

Contents

ABIDING LOVE ....

ALL GOD'S CHILDREN ....

AMAZING GRACE ....

BEAUTIFUL ISLE OF SOMEWHERE ....

BEYOND THE SUNSET ....

BLESS HIS HOLY NAME ....

CLAP YOUR HANDS ....

ETERNAL LIFE ....

(AN) EVENING PRAYER ....

EVERYTHING IS BEAUTIFUL ....

FAITH OF OUR FATHERS ....

(THE) FAMILY OF GOD ....

(THE) FIRST THING I DO EVERY MORNING ....

FOR THOSE TEARS I DIED ....

FREELY, FREELY ....

GET ALL EXCITED ....

GREATER IS HE THAT IS IN ME 4

HE'S EVERYTHING TO ME 4

HE'S GOT THE WHOLE WORLD IN HIS HANDS 5

HE'S ONLY A PRAYER AWAY 5

HE'S STILL THE KING OF KINGS 5

HIS EYE IS ON THE SPARROW 4

HOLY, HOLY 6

I ASKED THE LORD 6

I FOUND THE ANSWER 6

I LOVE TO TELL THE STORY 6

I LOVE YOU WITH THE LOVE OF THE LORD 7

I NEVER WALK ALONE 7

I WILL SERVE THEE 7

I WOULD BE LIKE JESUS 7

IN THE GARDEN 7

IN THE UPPER ROOM 8

Contents

JUST A CLOSER WALK WITH THEE 82

JUST AS I AM 84

KUM BA YAH 86

(THE) LAST MILE OF THE WAY 88

(THE) LORD IS MY SHEPHERD 90

(THE) LORD'S PRAYER 92

LOVEST THOU ME (MORE THAN THESE?) 94

(A) MIGHTY FORTRESS IS OUR GOD 96

(A) MIRACLE HAPPENED TO ME 98

MY FAITH STILL HOLDS 100

MY TRIBUTE 102

NEARER MY GOD, TO THEE 85

NO ONE UNDERSTANDS LIKE JESUS 106

NOW I BELONG TO JESUS 108

O PERFECT LOVE 110

OH HAPPY DAY 112

OH PROMISE ME 117

(THE) OLD RUGGED CROSS 120

ONE GOD 114

PASS IT ONE 122

(A) PERFECT HEART 124

SOMEBODY BIGGER THAN YOU AND I 128

STAND UP, STAND UP FOR JESUS 127

TEACH ME TO PRAY 139

THEN CAME JESUS 142

TOMORROW 144

UPON THIS ROCK 148

(THE) VICTOR 130

WHAT A FRIEND WE HAVE IN JESUS 152

WHEN I KNEEL DOWN TO PRAY 156

WHEN GOD IS NEAR 154

WHISPERING HOPE 158

ABIDING LOVE

Words and Music by
Gloria Roe

REFRAIN

A-bid-ing love, the great-est sto-ry ev-er, Can fill each heart if o-pened to His call; So love Him now, this love He'll nev-er sev-er, A-bid-ing love from Him, Who's o-ver all.____

1.

2. No great-er Him, Who's o-ver all.____

ALL GOD'S CHILDREN

Words by William J. Gaither
and Charles Millhuff
Music by William J. Gaither

REFRAIN

All ___ God's chil-dren, ___ All ___ God's chil-dren, ___ All ___ God's chil-dren, ___ To be God's chil-dren, You've got-ta be born a gain! ___

If you think you can make it by go-in' to church, then

AMAZING GRACE

Adapted by Willis I

ETERNAL LIFE

Words and Music by
Olive Dungan and
St. Francis of Assisi

Lord, make me an in-stru-ment of Thy peace.

Where there is ha-tred, let me sow love; Where there is in-jur-y,

par-don; Where there is doubt, faith; Where there is de-spair,

BEAUTIFUL ISLE OF SOMEWHERE

Lyric by Jessie B. Pounds
Music by John S. Fearis

1. Some-where the sun is shin - ing, some-where the song - birds
2. Some-where the day is long - er, some-where the task is

dwell,_____ Hush, then, thy sad re - pin - ing,
done,_____ Some-where the heart is strong - er,

God lives, and all____ is well._____ Some - where, some - where.
Some-where the guer - don won._____

* Small notes for Vocal Duet

BEYOND THE SUNSET

Words by Virgil P. Brock
Music by Blanche Kerr Brock

1. Be - yond the sun - set, O bliss - ful morn - ing, When with our
2. Be - yond the sun - set no clouds will gath - er, No storms will
3. Be - yond the sun - set a hand will guide me To God, the
4. Be - yond the sun - set, O glad re - un - ion, With our dear

Sav - iour heav'n is be - gun.___ Earth's toil - ing end - ed O glo - rious
threat - en, no fears an - noy;___ O day of glad - ness, O day un -
Fa - ther, whom I a - dore;___ His glo - rious pres - ence, His words of
loved ones who've gone be - fore;___ In that fair home - land we'll know no

dawn-ing;   Be-yond the sun - set,   when day is   done.
end - ed,   Be-yond the sun - set,   e - ter-nal   joy!
wel - come,   Will be my por - tion   on that fair   shore.
part-ing,   Be-yond the sun - set   for-ev-er - more!

W.C. POOLE

SUNRISE

B.D. ACKLEY

Sun-rise to - mor-row,   sun-rise to - mor-row, Sun-rise in

glo - ry is   wait-ing for   me;   Sun-rise to - mor-row,

sun-rise to - mor - row, Sun-rise with Je-sus for e - ter - ni - ty.

BLESS HIS HOLY NAME

Words and Music by
Andraé Crouch

CLAP YOUR HANDS

Words and Music by
Jimmy Owens

21

AN EVENING PRAYER

Words and Music by
C.M. Battersby and
Charles H. Gabriel

1. If I have wound-ed an - y soul to-day, If I have caused one foot to go a - stray, If I have walked in my own will - ful way, Dear
2. If I have ut - tered i - dle word or vain, If I have turned a - side from want or pain, Lest I of - fend some oth - er thru the strain, Dear
3. If I have been per - verse or hard, or cold, If I have longed for shel - ter in thy fold, When Thou has giv - en me some fort to hold, Dear

FREELY, FREELY

Words and Music by
Carol Owens

Gently Flowing

God for

gave my sin in Je - sus' name, I've been
(2.) pow'r is giv'n in Je - sus' name, in____

born a - gain in Je - sus' name; And in
earth and heav'n in Je - sus' name; And in

EVERYTHING IS BEAUTIFUL

Words and Music by
Ray Stevens

29

Verse 2: We shouldn't care about the length of his hair or the color of his skin
Don't worry about what shows from without but the love that lives within
We gonna get it all together now and everything gonna work out fine
Just take a little time to look on the good side my friend and straighten it out in your mind.

FAITH OF OUR FATHERS

Moderately

Adapted by Willis Ra

Faith of our fa - thers! liv - ing still
Our fa - thers, chained in pris - ons dark,
Faith of our fa - thers! we will love

In spite of dun - geon, fire, and sword,
Were still in heart and con - science free;
Both friend and foe in all our strife,

O how our hearts beat high with joy
How sweet would be their chil - dren's fate
And preach thee, too as love knows how

THE FAMILY OF GOD

Words and Music by
William J. Gaither and Gloria Gaither

Intro.

Chorus

I'm so glad I'm a part of the fam-'ly of God! I've been washed in the foun-tain, Cleansed by His blood. Joint heirs with Je - sus as we tra - vel this sod, For I'm part of the fam-'ly, the fam-'ly of God. God.

1 Going on 2 Fine

THE FIRST THING I DO EVERY MORNING

Words and Music by
Johnny Lange, Evelyn Merrill,
and Eddie Ballantine

FOR THOSE TEARS I DIED

Words and Music by
Marsha J. Stevens

REFRAIN

Je - sus said, "Come to the wa - ter, stand by My___ side. I know you are thir - sty; you won't be de - nied.___ I felt ev - 'ry tear - drop when in dark - ness you cried;_____ _____ And I strove to re - mind you that for those tears I died. 2. Your died. 3. ___

GET ALL EXCITED

Words and Music by
William J. Gaither

39

HIS EYE IS ON THE SPARROW

Words and Music by
Charles H. Gabriel

43

GREATER IS HE THAT IS IN ME

Words and Music by
Lanny Wolfe

46

HE'S EVERYTHING TO ME

Words and Music by
Ralph Carmichael

Till by faith I met Him face to face, And I felt the won-der

of His grace, Then I knew that He was more than just a

God who didn't care, That lived a - way out there and Now He walks be-side me

HE'S GOT THE WHOLE WORLD
IN HIS HANDS

Adapted by Willis R:

HE'S ONLY A PRAYER AWAY

Words and Music by
Johnny Lange and
Harold L. Graham

1. There's some-one who loves ev-'ry sin-ner. _____ He's
2. Though friends may de-ride and for-sake you, _____ And
3. Our Lord suf-fered death for trans-gres-sion, _____ The
4. When o-thers for-sake and de-sert you, _____ 'And

call-ing, oh hear him to-day, _____ 'Tis Je-sus our
leave you a-lone in the way, _____ Re-mem-ber the
death that each mor-tal should pay, _____ Oh, why do you
you're in the depth of des-pair, _____ Let God share your

bles-sed Re-deem-er, _____
prom-ise of Je-sus, _____
lang-uish in sor-row, _____
bur-den and sor-row, _____ HE'S ON-LY A PRAYER A-WAY. _____
Just seek Him and He'll be there. _____

57

CHORUS

HE'S ON-LY A PRAYER A - WAY, _____ HE'S

ON - LY A PRAYER A - WAY. _____

God will be with you when ev - er you pray. HE'S

ON - LY A PRAYER A - WAY. _____

EXTRA VERSES

- 5 -
Though you walk alone in the darkness
You're lost and there's nothin' in sight
He's with you each step of the journey
He's there with His guiding light.

- 6 -
You followed the path of a sinner
Temptation had led you astray
Remember He'll always forgive you
If you"ll only meet him halfway.

- 7 -
He has an infinite power
And so many things He can do
He'll always be ready to help you
Just ask Him to come to you.

- 8 -
Whenever you feel sad and lonely
'Cause all of your hopes fell apart
He'll bring you a new life if only
You'll keep Him within your heart.

HE'S STILL THE KING OF KINGS

Words by Gloria & William J. Gaither
Music by William J. Gaither

1. In the hills of Ju - de - a the lone shep - herds
walked by the grave - sides of earth's fall - en
rode thro' the ci - ty, the crowd claimed Him
sound of the trum - pet, the skies blaze with

watch; Hope is gone, there is no call for sing - ing;
kings, Who op - posed Him and yet He's still reign - ing!
King; Thou-sands cheered Him and the streets filled with sing - ing;
fire; Moun - tains thun - der with God's judg - ment sing - ing;

60

I ASKED THE LORD

Words and Music by
Johnny Lange and Jimmy Duncan

62

I thank the Lord for ev-'ry-thing, and I count my bless-ings each day; He came to me when I need-ed Him, I on-ly had to pray; And He'll come to you if you ask Him to, He's on-ly a prayer a-way!

HOLY, HOLY

Words and Music by
Jimmy Owens

1. Ho - ly, ho - ly, ho - ly, ho - ly, Ho - ly,
(2.) Fa - ther, gra - cious Fa - ther, We're so
(3.) Je - sus, pre - cious Je - sus, We're so
(4.) Spir - it, Ho - ly Spir - it, Come and
(5.) Ho - ly, ho - ly, ho - ly, Ho - ly,
(6.) lu - jah, hal - le - lu - jah, Hal - le -

ho - ly, Lord God Al - might - y; And we
blest to be your chil - dren, gra - cious Fa - ther; And we
glad that You've re - deemed us, pre - cious Je - sus; And we
fill our hearts a - new, Ho - ly Spir - it; And we
ho - ly, Lord God Al - might - y; And we
lu - jah, hal - le - lu - jah; And we

lift our hearts be - fore You as a to - ken of our love, Ho - ly, ho - ly, ho - ly,
lift our heads be - fore You as a to - ken of our love, Gra - cious Fa - ther, gracious
lift our hands be - fore You as a to - ken of our love, Pre - cious Je - sus, pre - cious
lift our voice be - fore You as a to - ken of our love, Ho - ly Spir - it, Ho - ly
lift our hearts be - fore You as a to - ken of our love, Ho - ly, ho - ly, ho - ly,
lift our hearts be - fore You as a to - ken of our love, Hal - le - lu - jah, hal - le -

ho - ly.
Fa - ther.
Je - sus.
Spir - it.
ho - ly.
lu - jah.

2. Gra - cious
3. Pre - cious
4. Ho - ly
5. Ho - ly,
6. Hal - le -

rit.

I FOUND THE ANSWER

Words and Music by
Johnny Lange

67

I LOVE TO TELL THE STORY

Words and Music by
Katherine Hankey and
William G. Fischer

69

I LOVE YOU WITH THE LOVE OF THE LORD

Words and Music by
Jim Gilbert

I NEVER WALK ALONE

Words and Music by
A. H. Ackley

1. I nev-er walk a-lone, I have a Sav-iour, Who
2. I nev-er walk a-lone, in storm-y weath-er, When

walks be-side me ev-'ry-where I go; My heart re-joic-es in His lov-ing
winds of trou-ble sweep a-bout my head. I know I'm safe, be-cause we are to-

I WILL SERVE THEE

Words and Music by
Gloria and William J. Gaither

Lyrics:
I will serve Thee_____ be-cause I love Thee_____ You have giv-en life to me_____ I was nothing_____ be-fore You found me_____ You have giv-en

I WOULD BE LIKE JESUS

Words and Music by
B. D. Ackley and
James Rowe

IN THE GARDEN

Words and Music by
C. Austin Miles

IN THE UPPER ROOM

Words and Music by
William J. Gaither

1. There's a place for all the weak and wea - ry, A_____ place where all may find real peace._____ _____ In the up-per room with Je - sus, _____ All our cares and heart - aches cease._____

2. (There is) cool - ing wa-ter for the wea - ry, There's a balm for ev - 'ry bro - ken heart._____ There is rest for all the heav - y la - den, His peace to you He will im - part._____

JUST A CLOSER WALK WITH THEE

Adapted by Willis Ray

1. I am weak but Thou art strong, _____ Je sus,
2. Through this world of toil and snares, _____ If I
3. When the jour - ney here is o'er, _____ Time for

keep me from all wrong. _____ I'll be sat - is - fied as
fal - ter, Lord, who cares? _____ Who with me my bur - den
me will be no more. _____ Guide me to Thy dis - tant

long _____ As I walk, let me walk close to Thee. _____
shares? _____ None but Thee, dear Lord, none but Thee. _____
shore. _____ To Thy shore, Oh dear Lord, to Thy shore. _____

83

JUST AS I AM

By Charlotte Elliot and
William B. Bradbury

NEARER MY GOD, TO THEE

Words and Music by
Sarah F. Adams and
Lowell Mason

KUM BA YAH

Adapted by Willi

THE LAST MILE OF THE WAY

Words and Music by
Johnson Oatman, Jr.
and Wm. Edie Marks

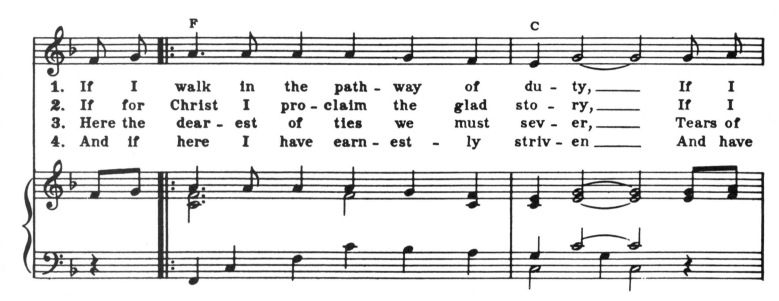

1. If I walk in the path - way of du - ty, _____ If I
2. If for Christ I pro - claim the glad sto - ry, _____ If I
3. Here the dear - est of ties we must sev - er, _____ Tears of
4. And if here I have earn - est - ly striv - en _____ And have

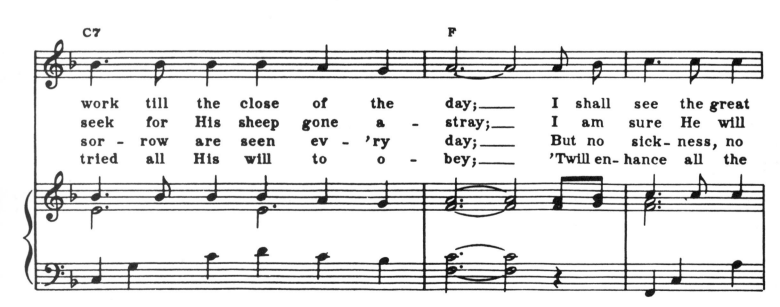

work till the close of the day; _____ I shall see the great
seek for His sheep gone a - stray; _____ I am sure He will
sor - row are seen ev - 'ry day; _____ But no sick - ness, no
tried all His will to o - bey; _____ 'Twill en - hance all the

THE LORD IS MY SHEPHERD

Words and Music by
James Montgomery and
Thomas Koschat

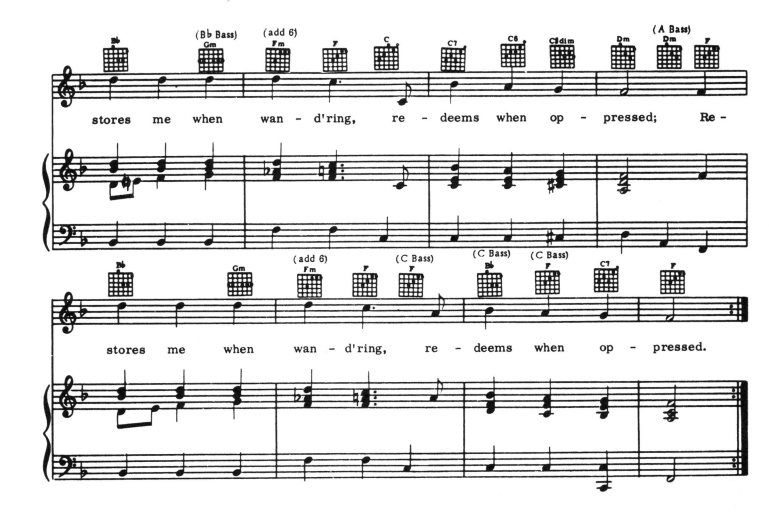

2. Thro' the valley and shadow of death though I stray,
Since Thou art my guardian, no evil I fear;
Thy rod shall defend me, Thy staff be my stay;
No harm can befall with My Comforter near;
No harm can befall with My Comforter near.

3. In the midst of affliction my table is spread;
With blessings unmeasured my cup runneth o'er;
With perfume and oil Thou anointest my head;
O what shall I ask of Thy providence more?
O what shall I ask of Thy providence more?

4. Let goodness and mercy, my bountiful God,
Still follow my steps till I meet Thee above;
I seek by the path which my fore-fathers trod,
Thro' the land of their sojourn, Thy kingdom of love;
Thro' the land of their sojourn, Thy kingdom of love.

THE LORD'S PRAYER

By FELIX MENDELSSOHN

LOVEST THOU ME (More Than These?)

Words and Music by
William J. Gaither

A MIGHTY FORTRESS IS OUR GOD

Words and Music by
Martin Luther

A MIRACLE HAPPENED TO ME (It Could Happen To You)

Words by Johnny Lange
Music by Ben Weisman

MY FAITH STILL HOLDS

Words and Music by
William J. and Gloria Gaither

CHORUS

MY TRIBUTE

Words and Music by
Andraé Crouch

How_____ can I say thanks for the

things   You have done   for me?   Things_____ so un - de

104

NO ONE UNDERSTANDS LIKE JESUS

Words and Music by
John W. Peterson

1. No one un-der-stands like Je-sus, He's a friend be-yond com-pare;
2. No one un-der-stands like Je-sus, Ev-'ry woe He sees and feels;
3. No one un-der-stands like Je-sus, When the foes of life as-sail;
4. No one un-der-stands like Je-sus, When you falt-er on the way;

Meet Him at the throne of mer-cy, He is wait-ing for you there.
Ten-der-ly He whis-pers com-fort, And the bro-ken heart He heals.
You should nev-er be dis-cour-aged, Je-sus cares and will not fail.
Tho' you fail Him, sad-ly fail Him, He will par-don you to-day.

NOW I BELONG TO JESUS

O PERFECT LOVE

By D. F. BLOOMFIELD
and J. BARNEY

OH HAPPY DAY

Based on the
Doddridge-Rimbault hymn
Adapted by Willis Ray

ONE GOD

Words and Music by
Ervin Drake and James Shirl

Slowly

Voice *(with much expression)*

Mil - lions of stars placed in the skies by ONE GOD!

ONE GOD! Mil - lions of men lift up their eyes to ONE GOD!

ONE GOD! So man - y child - ren cal - ling to Him by

Walk with me, Broth - er; there were no Stran-gers af - ter His work wa

done, For your God *(optional) Your God* and my God

my God are One.

One.

OH PROMISE ME

Words and Music by
Clement Scott and
R. De Koven

Oh, prom-ise me that some day you and I Will take our love to-geth-er to some sky

Where we can be a - lone, and faith re - new, And

find the hol-lows where those flow-ers grew,_____ Those first sweet vi-o-lets of ear - ly spring,which

THE OLD RUGGED CROSS

Words and Music by
George Bennard

1. On a hill far a-way stood an old rug-ged cross, The em-blem of suf-f'ring and shame, And I love that old cross where the
2. Oh, that old rug-ged cross, so de-spised by the world, Has a won-drous at-trac-tion for me, For the dear Lamb of God left His
3. In the old rug-ged cross, stained with blood so di-vine, A won-drous beau-ty I see; For 'twas on that old cross Je-sus
4. To the old rug-ged cross I will ev-er be true, Its shame and re-proach glad-ly bear; Then He'll call me, some day, to my

PASS IT ON

Words and Music by
Kurt Kaiser

1. It

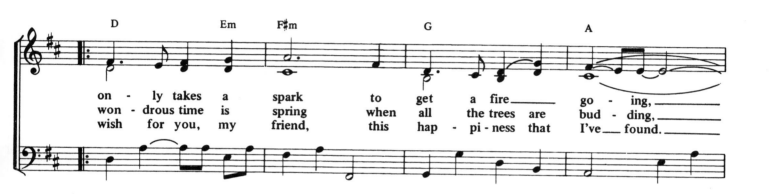

on - ly takes a spark to get a fire_____ go - ing, _____
won - drous time is spring when all the trees are bud - ding, _____
wish for you, my friend, this hap - pi - ness that I've_____ found. _____

_____ And soon all those a - round can warm up in its
The birds be - gin to sing, the flow - ers start their
You can de - pend on Him; it mat - ters not where

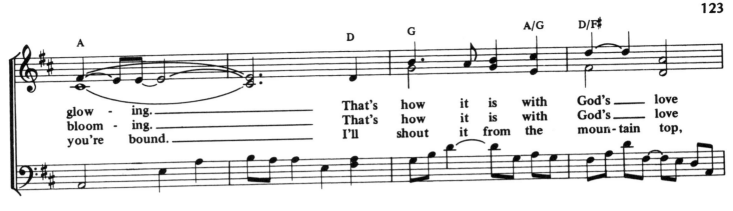

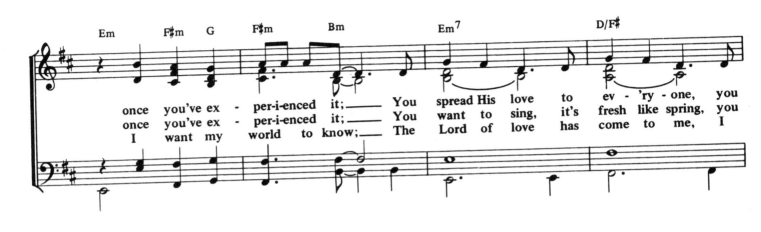

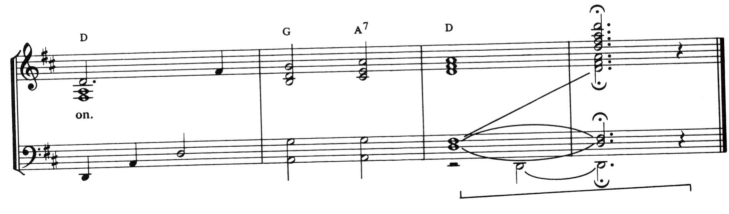

A PERFECT HEART

Words and Music by
Reba Rambo and Dony McGuire

126

STAND UP, STAND UP FOR JESUS

Words and Music by
George Duffield and
George J. Webb

Bright

Stand up! Stand up for Je - sus, ye sol - dier of the

cross! Lift high His roy - al ban - ner, it must not suf - fer

loss. From vic - t'ry un - to vic - t'ry His ar - my shall He

lead,—— Till ev - 'ry foe is van-quished and Christ is Lord in deed.

SOMEBODY BIGGER THAN YOU AND I

Words and Music by
Johnny Lange, Hy Heath
and Sonny Burke

THE VICTOR

Words and Music by
Jamie Owens-Collins

136

138

TEACH ME TO PRAY

**Music by
JESSIE MAE JEWITT
and Lyric by
GEORGE GRAFF JR.**

THEN JESUS CAME

Words by Oswald J. Smith
Music by Homer Rodeheaver

VERSE

1. One sat a - lone   be - side the high - way beg - ging,   His eyes were
2. From home and friends   the e - vil spir - its drove him,   A - mong the
3. "Un - clean! un - clean!"   the lep - er cried in tor - ment,   The deaf, the
4. So men to - day   have found the Sav - iour a - ble,   They could not

blind,   the light he could not see;   He clutched his rags   and shiv-ered in the
tombs   he dwelt in mis - er - y;   He cut him - self   as de-mon pow'rs pos-
dumb,   in help-less-ness stood near;   The fe - ver raged,   dis-ease had gripped its
con - quer pas-sion, lust and sin;   Their bro-ken hearts   had left them sad and

143

TOMORROW

Words and Music by
Carvin Winans and Deborah Winans

147

UPON THIS ROCK

Words and Music by
Gloria Gaither and Dony McGuire

WHAT A FRIEND WE HAVE IN JESUS

Adapted by Willis Ray

153

WHEN GOD IS NEAR

Words and Music
A. H. Ackl

1. When God is near, with light my path is glow-ing, The cup of life with
2. When God is near the heav-y load is lift-ed, And ev-'ry du-ty
3. When God is near the tempt-er can-not lure me, The peace of God sur-

glad-ness o-ver-flows, And in the gar-den of my heart is
charms me with de-light; The clouds of sor-row by His love are
pass-ing sweet is mine; "Joint heir with Christ," His mer-cies re-as-

grow-ing The flow'r of love more fra-grant than the sweet-est rose.
rift-ed, And songs of joy my soul keeps sing-ing in the night.
sure me, And some day I shall dwell with Him in realms di-vine.

WHEN I KNEEL DOWN TO PRAY

Words and Music by
B. D. Ackley and
A. H. Ackley

Some-how the

1. Sav - ior seems a lit - tle near - er,
(2.) place of qui - et med - i - ta - tion, When I kneel down to
(3.) there with Christ a lit - tle long - er,

And fel - low - ship with Him a lit - tle dear - er,
pray, _____ In - creas - es all the joy of that re - la - tion, When
And rise to face the world a lit - tle strong - er,

CHORUS

WHISPERING HOPE

Words and Music by
Alice Hawthorne

* Small notes for Vocal Duet